A PORTABLE PARADISE

PRAISE FOR A PORTABLE PARADISE

With *A Portable Paradise*, Roger Robinson shows us that he can be the voice of our communal consciousness, while at the same time always subverting, playing and beguiling with his beautiful verse.

— Afua Hirsch

* * *

"It is the job of Paradise
to comfort those who've been left behind"

Grenfell was an event so devastating many of us struggled to find the words for it, so what better time to turn to one of the most prominent voices in Caribbean-British poetry. I would go as far to say Robinson is one of the most important poetic voices in the UK right now. There are poems here that broke me and I cried all over again for the victims of Grenfell, but as I read on, I was pulled through other voices, all carrying the rage and pain of their history. Reading these poems I got to meditate on Sade, Bob Marley and Stuart Hall, but also a nurse called Grace who "sang pop songs on her shift, like they were hymns"; I got to read the prayers of a father for his son. This is the role of any great poet, to honour the best and hardest part of living so they can give us a language for what we have in us that makes survival possible.

— Raymond Antrobus

* * *

There is poetry and then there is Roger Robinson. That is all. From the moment I first met him until now the passion and craft for the pen remains the same. A master wordsmith, one of the last true poets.

— Charlie Dark

ROGER ROBINSON

A PORTABLE PARADISE

PEEPAL TREE

First published in Great Britain in 2019
Reprinted 2020
Peepal Tree Press Ltd
17 King's Avenue
Leeds LS6 1QS
UK

ISBN 13: 9781845234331

Supported by
ARTS COUNCIL
ENGLAND

ACKNOWLEDGEMENTS

"Stubbs Whistlejacket" was a commission from the National Portrait Gallery and also appears in the book *George Stubbs: "all done from Nature"*; "Ascension" appeared in *One for the Trouble: Book Slam Annual*, Vol. 1 (ed. Patrick Neate); "The Human Canvas" appeared in *Red: Contemporary Black British Poetry* (Peepal Tree Press); "Repast" appeared in *Filigree: Contemporary Black British Poetry* (Peepal Tree Press); "The Ever Changing Dot" was a commission from the Institute of International Visual Arts; "The Missing" was commissioned for Africa Writes: R.A.P. Party.

For friendship, guidance , support and encouragement:

Suzanne Alleyne, Raymond Antrobus, Francesca Beard, Sharmilla Beezmohun, Malika Booker, Marc Boothe, Zakia Carpenter-Hall, Nicholas Chapman, Nicky Crabb, Charlie Dark, Kwame Dawes, Inua Ellams, Bernardine Evaristo, Piers Faccini, Arlette George, Jan Gleichmar, Colin Grant, Sami Al Haj, Elontra Hall, Afua Hirsch, Kiki Hitomi, Anthony Joseph, Peter Kahn, Tobi Kyeremateng, Jacob Sam-La Rose, Kevin Le Gendre, Nick Makoha, Kevin Martin, Lisa Mead, Vidal Montgomery, Nii Ayikwei Parkes, Johny Pitts, Will Power, Rob Rainbow, Dean Ricketts, Isele Robinson-Cooper, Sarah Sanders, Nathalie Teitler, Marla Teyolia, Grace Williams, Imani Wilson.

Apples and Snakes, Beatfreeks, The Arts Council of England, The Complete Works, Jeremy Poynting, Hannah Bannister and all the hardworking team at Peepal Tree Press.

Cover photograph by Johny Pitts
Cover design by Nicola Griffiths

For My Beautiful Family, Nicola and Caden.

CONTENTS

III

IV

V

THE MISSING

For the victims of the Grenfell Tower fire disaster

As if their bodies became lighter,
ten of those seated
in front pews began to float,
and then to lie down as if on
a bed. Then pass down the aisle,
as if on a conveyor belt of pure air,
slow as a funeral cortege,
past the congregants, some sinking
to their knees in prayer.
One woman, rocking back and forth,
muttered, *What about me Lord,*
why not me?

The Risen stream slowly, so slowly
out the gothic doors
and up to the sky, finches darting
deftly between them.

Ten streets away,
a husband tries to hold onto the feet
of his floating wife. At times her force
lifts him slightly off the ground,
his grip slipping. He falls
to his knees with just her high-
heeled shoe in his hand.
He shields and squints his eyes
as she is backlit by the sun.

A hundred people start floating
from the windows of a tower block;
from far enough away they could be
black smoke from spreading flames.

A father with his child on top his shoulders;
men in sandcoloured galiibeas; a woman
with an Elvis quiff and vintage glasses,
a deep indigo hijab flapping in the wind;
an artist in a wax-cloth headwrap:
all airborne, these superheroes,
this airborne pageantry of faith,
this flock of believers.

Amongst the cirrus clouds, floating like hair,
they begin to look like a separate city.
Someone looking on could mistake them
for new arrivants to earth.
They are the city of the missing.
We, now, the city of the stayed.

HAIBUN FOR THE LOOKERS

The people on the ground look up at the burning building,
their faces illuminated by the glow of fire-ash floating gently down.
Pieces of burning building fall like giant sparks from a welder's torch,
then a flaming fire-snake slides its way from the fourth floor
straight to the top. In the lights of mobile phones,
shadows wave makeshift flags, until they no longer wave them
and their silhouette fades to the roaring fiery light.

The spectacle's now more like a painting of a building on fire than an
actual fire: black velvet night rippling orange-yellow and punch-red
acrylic flames.

The lookers are imagining their settees in flames, their orange floral
wallpaper slowly bubbling up and bursting like blisters before giving
in to a blackened charred heat. Then the swan dive of a few bodies.
Some sob for their own, some sob for others, some just sob.
The soot in the air burns in the noses of onlookers. Smoke makes
some wheeze in the branched bronchiole of their lungs, from when
they were in the building, then not totally on fire, but from corridors
of smoke, when they edged blindly towards the stairwell, hoping not
to walk into fire.

The sky's darker now as background to the flame,
the smoke rising like an offering of burning sage.
The building has become a charred black tomb,
and the sky looks down on us saying what's lost is lost,
gather what is left and build new lives.

As for the onlookers, whose numbers have swelled, this is what they'll
remember: the floating ash and flaming debris, bodies in flight and
bodies in shadow, the smoke leaving discreetly into the night sky,
clouds at night and the snake, the giant snake of flaming fire.

The heat at my back,
I throw my baby out the window.
Catch him Lord!

FOURTEEN TO ONE

As the building burned
I tied fourteen pastel
bedsheets into sturdy
knots and climbed out
the window. The fifteenth
sheet was to tie my daughter
to my back as we went down.

THE PORTRAIT MUSEUM

The morning after, the streets filled with portraits
of missing people – brothers with bushy beards,

olive-skinned, wrinkle-faced grandmothers,
pig-tailed daughters with red ribbons, smiling –

stuck on tree trunks, walls and fence boards,
the neon red MISSING floating above their heads.

In a minute of pure clairvoyance we understand
that many of these pictures are the faces of the dead,

some looking like they were saying the word goodbye
as the picture was shot at a family gathering.

Without sleep, some struggle to keep their posters
straight, stop the sellotape sticking to itself.

These were the flimsy paper faces of hope for the living;
those not taped well are blown away on the breeze.

Many with posters refuse this first day of mourning;
as days went on, the wind blew most of them away.

BLAME

The building burned,
so the council blamed the contractors
who shredded all the papers;
so the contractors blamed
health and safety for passing
all the required tests;
so the prime minister
came, saw and left,
and talked to no one
and shook no one's hand.
Meantime its tenants are left
to grieve in sterile hotels,
with nothing to bury but ash,
and survivors walk like zombies
trying not to look up
at the charred gravestone.
People still cry.
Nobody took the blame.

THE FATHER

This twelve-year-old girl, doing an interview on the TV about her father being missing after the fire, is becoming her father. She is already head and shoulders above her mother who stands behind her, red-rimmed eyes darting with worry. Note when the interviewer asks how she feels, the daughter starts becoming her father. She concentrates her answer on the actions she must take, the things that are directly within her control. Days later she will fill in the forms necessary for them to get new housing. She will wake up her mother, weak with grief, and bring to her bed fattet hummus and makdous with olive oil and za'tar. She will make her mother have a shower in the morning and comb her mother's hair and lay her clothes on the bed. She has taken to reading several newspapers while drinking strong cardamom-flavoured coffee while Umm Kulthum is singing about her heart on the radio.

GHOSTS

You feel it as soon as you settle in your new flat, perhaps when you are making rocket salad with lemon dressing; the smell of el ras hanout and cumin will assail your nose, make you think for a minute. You'll turn on a light and your hand will carry a faint scent of cocoa butter. You'll come home from the office and a young woman in a rust-coloured hijab, barefoot in mint pyjamas, whom you've never met before, will agitatedly ask the way out, but by the time you point she'll have disappeared. Interrupting your evening's Netflix selection, you hear the feet of at least six small children tramping overhead. The copper taps in your refurbished rooms run smoke for a few seconds before flowing with water. Your weekend lover says he'd rather you stay over at his place and gives you no reason. You'll find yourself making up reasons to stay late at the office or catch a drink with friends.

At night a roaring heat will break you into sweat, and no matter how you try you can't wake up and you can't breathe. You'll hear a call to prayer mixed in with Fela Kuti's "Zombie" and a five-year-old girl constantly screaming for help from the guttural part of her voice and you'll sit in the darkness for a while clasping your knees, looking out your extra large window at the view you've paid so dearly for.

DOPPELGANGER

A week after the building burned
I saw my dead wife; she smiled at me.

Right now its hard for me
to tell the living from the dead.

My wedding ring is sinking
into my swollen finger.

There is pressure building there;
but I do not want to use soap to slide it off.

Even though she is dead
I am still married to her.

I see children playing
who look like my wife when she was young.

I knew my wife when she was young.
I wanted to talk to her, this woman

who looked liked my wife;
I wanted to hold her

but what I really wanted was my wife,
who is dead.

As I trace my thumb
over the silver ring.

DOLLS

If I could, like the gods of fate, somehow rearrange the events, I would start with Muhammed's fridge that exploded and started the fire. I would give Muhammed some clue that all was not right with it – perhaps his hummus goes off prematurely or the water collects under the vegetable crisper. Something to make Muhammed replace the fridge. Then I would give those who died on the top floors a reason not to be home. I would have had the fire on the day of Carnival and encouraged those on the top floors be a part of the festivities. I'd let the husbands who left their wives and families home to earn some money on night shifts or driving cabs find a little extra money in their accounts, so that night they'd have taken their children out for shawarma and orange juice down Marble Arch, while they smoked shisha and talked about how good their lives felt. All the children who died would have visited their grandparents that day, here or abroad. I'd make the cladding that burned like dry straw be fireproofed to international standards; let life and love continue in Grenfell.

BOYS LIGHT FIREWORKS ON THE GROUND FLOOR
OF GARDINER HOUSE ESTATE

They light the fireworks
like candles on a birthday
cake they've never had.

THE JOB OF PARADISE

It is the job of Paradise
to comfort those who've been left behind,

to think that all those loved and lost
would live on there like tiny gods.

It is the job of mumbled prayers
to help you calm your hurts and fears.

It is the job of the long black hearse
to show we head to death from birth.

It is the job of a clean neat grave
to remind us how to live our days.

If only I could live my days till death suffice
and make Earth feel like Paradise.

II

(SOME) SWEAT

Catching a fever in the hull of the slave-
ship, he became drenched. Sweat dripping
off his face like tears.

In the sugarcane field with a machete
he thought about how it would feel to
hack the master's throat like the tender
necks of these canes, as beads of sweat
rolled down his knuckles and wet
the silvered edge of his blade.

As they whipped him it wasn't the pain
of the stroke that hurt, but the salt of his own
sweat seeping into his wounds that made
him cry out.

As the mistress rode him in the night
her sweat would sometimes fall into his eyes
and in his mouth, leaving him salty
with her aftertaste.

The night he ran he could hear
the barking dogs behind him,
and he ran till his cotton shirt
could hold no more sweat.

WOKE

I woke up in chains in the belly of the slave ship. The dip of the bow and the moan of the timbers made me fall asleep. When I woke again I was being whipped to get up. I passed out and when I woke I was on an auction block as men with ashy fingers checked my teeth. With a neck iron digging into my skin, I walked till I collapsed and when I woke the neck iron had become a noose which they pulled until I choked. I saw them looking at me, even little white kids pointing till it all went black. I woke up being sprayed to the floor with police hoses and dogs snapping at my shins. As the dog sank its teeth in my calf, a police hit me with his baton until I passed out. I woke up on the 16th floor of a tower block looking out the window with a clear view of the land that does not belong to me.

BLACK ANTHURIUM

(From an historical fact told to me by Professor Oswald Glean Chase of Howard University)

You couldn't be more priapic;
you confront us with your sexuality,
like you faced the convicted
white French women
who were given a choice: have sex
with the strongest black slave
and bear a child into slavery,
or be imprisoned for life back in France.
So many questions.
Who buys this flower and in
what circumstance or event?
Its eroticism surely overshadows
any other sentiment.
What a binary to be faced with,
and what thoughts rushed through the minds
of the French women?
What thoughts did the slave have –
and who nursed the clay-skinned babies?
Did anyone fall in love with the babies,
the slave or the French women?
See how your reproduction is assured
by the deep black gleaming skin
of your heart-shaped leaf,
by spreading seed or cuttings.

See their descendants in Sangre Grande
and Arima: short-tempered, smart and strong.
The legacy of genetic breeding
bobbing up and down in the breeze.
You must adapt to new environments.
You must produce new flowers.

SLAVERY LIMERICK

Bill was a slave from Nantucket
who stole a bearskin and a musket.
He heard *Stop where you stand
put up both of your hands*.
But he zigged-zagged and ran
and said *Fuck it*.

WINDRUSH

They came down from the ship
on a footbridge of firewood,

architectural pleats in their trousers
and suitcases each containing a live lizard.

Eventually they'd put away
their bowties of cut banana leaves

and take to drinking sea-water shots down
the pub with beards of black smoke.

On the weekend they'd play bingo with passport
pages and levitate at night to basslines in the Mecca ballroom.

They'd eat their fried clay dumpling and salted
shark and don hat brims so sharp it could cut style,

with their twopence coin-button, double-breasted
jackets with pocket squares of betting slips.

But still the three wooden birds on their walls
were flying back home in super slow motion,

because nothing promised was what it seemed,
but it was somehow more than what they left.

BLACK OLIVE

I am introduced to a white woman at a literary party. I'm introduced to her as a writer and she is introduced to me as the director of a literary company. She picks up a black olive and says *Black olives are better than the rest aren't they. I love me some black olives* and she pops it into her mouth and suddenly I am in her mouth bouncing off the soft trampoline of her tongue. I have become miniaturised to the size of an olive floating on a wave of saliva skimming the tops of her teeth and tucked in to her cheek. Before I can get my bearings, from behind her cracked molar a voice says *Hi*. He is as dark as me and he says, *Don't tell me you're a writer, a novelist? No, poet*, I reply. *The black olive line?* I nod slowly. A wave of saliva nearly makes us lose our footing and another guy, darker skinned than both of us, comes sliding on his bum. He stands up. We all say *Hi.*

BOB MARLEY IN BRIXTON

He doesn't feel like Bob Marley. He doesn't feel like Bob Marley, the great reggae singer, as he walks down Brixton Market, looking for some saltfish, plantain and cassava. He does not feel at home. He is not at home. The market vendor wants to give him the food for free, but he still pays. He can still feel his wounds healing, just below his chest under the bandage. People are starting to notice him. He has to keep it moving. He heads back to his girlfriend's house in Chelsea. He does not want too much attention. He is wary of people right now. He cannot trust anyone. He smells of weed and coconut incense. His wife and family are back in Jamaica. You can't get this type of food in Chelsea. He gets a feeling for some peanut punch. As the seller throws the milk and the nuts into the blender, he's content to let the noise fill up the shop. The seller's saying something but Bob pretends he can't hear over the blender. He doesn't want to talk to anyone. He doesn't feel like one of the greatest musicians in the world. People start peeping in the patty shop. The seller tries to give Bob Marley the peanut punch for free. Bob Marley leaves the money on the counter anyway. He walks towards the station. No, he doesn't feel like Bob Marley because the old Bob Marley has to be reborn. If it's a war they want, then it's a war they'll get. A war of the spirit, a spiritual war. On his next album, he has to come back like a revolutionary. On the next album he's coming back with bullets and brimstone and fire.

BOTTLES FLYING IN SLOW MOTION AT THE POLICE

When you publicly
murder us, who will speak up for us
but these flying bottles?

BEWARE

When police place knees
at your throat, you may not live
to tell of choking.

IT SOON COME

Something settle here
in this town, on these streets,
something dark and gritty,
something acid, acrid.
Is de way the man dem stan up
screw face all day. Is de low talk
and raise eyebrow, stares
and slow nods. The heat
was close, too close, humid,
heavy with dread and in de market
the stench of rotting fish was high
and the fruit grew black spots.
People were saying, "It soon come"
without knowing what they were talking
'bout. Even the incense man
look worried, like he could feel it.
Nobody selling, nobody buying;
they walking up and down
like zombies, and all the cars
was driving real slow, like everyone
waiting on a signal. Some youths
on bmx's start pullin' up dey hoodies.
The town went quiet, hushed
but for the shatter of a smashed bottle.
Then came the faint smell of smoke
and the sky turned the colour of dust
and a helicopter, small as a fly,
hover over the festering wound.
In these streets, something settle here
something dark and gritty
something acid, acrid.
It soon come.

WALK WITH ME

I walk through Brixton with a young man
in screw-faced street mode,
and I tell him it's okay to relax.
His temptations course through his blood.
He calls me witness, he calls me bookish.
We walk avoiding certain streets,
Loughborough, the railway. We both know why.

I tell him that under these very streets we walk,
deep beneath the concrete, beneath the tarmac,
beneath the rubble, the dirt, and the rock,
there is a river flowing called Effra.
A black and powerful river coursing without light.
That one hundred and fifty years ago
royalty would sail down this river
in their best finery into Brixton
never thinking about crack, never thinking about cafés.

But every now and then
these towerblocks act like speakers
and the calming sound of a pure, flowing river
can be heard throughout Brixton's streets.
I tell him that even though the river calls,
things have moved on here.
Brixton is not its history,
and neither should we be
though we hear the call of the past.

ASHES TO FIRE

Beware of these hot nights in Brixton
when cabbies sit outside laughing
on homemade stools and charge
twice the going rate to get up,
and crackheads walk
with presidential purpose
to meet wincing dealers whose crack foils
rub against their fillings.
And somewhere up in the tracing paper
squares of light in the towerblocks,
grandmothers dice goat meat and season it
with curry spice and sweat, and a young man
stops brushing his fade in the mirror
and looks deep into the loose, light-brown threads
of his own eyes, while downstairs
in the car park a young father whispers
weed smoke about how his life feels,
like that burnt-out car that never moves,
the one with shattered windows
leaving diamond tears in the melting asphalt.
It's not too hot for bullet-proof vests velcroed
across their ribs, but it is too hot to sleep,
so the whole town is out. The fat rumpled staffies
are taking their hoodied boys for a walk.
Even the one-legged man is hopping down
the centre of the road, begging traffic
for revolution money. Out tonight,
too, are certain mans who don't take three steps
without looking backward
'cause they know their boy
who freestyles from his wheelchair,
let them Peckham mans come up
from behind with handguns,
.45s long nose, snub nose, trying to slump man.

Roll roll roll, watch, roll roll roll, watch.
Even a bus driver will kick your ass tonight
if you're trying to ride for free –
he's come up on road and tonight is too hot
to take shit. On hot nights like this
the pinpricks of sweat
could make mans remember old beef
that next mans forgot, and somebody
might get caught slipping with none
of his boys around and get bored up,
right there in the off license,
between the magazines and the special brew.
And a nine-year-old girl's spine
might take a stray bullet
so she may never skip to a beat
on concrete again. So beware,
beware of these hot nights in Brixton.

THE DARKENING RED OF YOUR BLOOD

Now your shoulders have broadened
and the cleft in the centre of your chest
is more pronounced,
at some point you will be stopped
by policemen for no valid reason.
They will ask unnecessary questions.
They will say something to try
to degrade you. They will look
for some reaction or excuse
to cause you some harm. Their eyes
will betray their intent and you will feel
an anger so mighty it will make you
clench your jaw, make the veins
in your temple's throb because you know
that with one punch of your youthful
strength you can lay them out like sleeping
infants, make them trace their maps of bruises
for weeks in the mirror. This is a trap,
young brother. Do not fall for it.
Don't be the ink of a new obituary.
Think about your mother's grimace,
think of the gap you'll leave
amongst your people, grieving
you like a tongue to a missing tooth.
Take the contempt out of your eyes.
They love the flow of blood;
it makes them feel powerful, like a god.
They'll talk about how dark red your blood
seemed at the station for years. They'll laugh
at its thickness, how you passed out begging
for help. Realise that keeping yourself alive
is bigger than racism and disrespect. Keep alive,
young brothers, keep living.

THERAPY

They are trying to get him to therapy, but he says it is not his way. He'd rather the fire burn in his head than in his stomach. If it is Allah's will, who is he to unload his burden on someone else. He opens his Quran to start his prayers.

I have come from Afghanistan where my father was killed and I lost contact. I have crossed deserts. I have lost my shoes. I've squeezed like a sardine in the rotting hull of a ship. I have doggy-paddled past floating bodies. I've been kicked in my back on a truck and spat blood until I, without a word of English, was thrown out on a motorway . You think this tower is the worst of my suffering? I am alive. It is Allah's will. I do not need your therapist. I need my prayers. Allah never gives you more than you can handle.

Endnote:
The Taliban killed his father in a spray of machine gun fire while his mother hid him under a bed. He was a teacher and they accused him of teaching anti-religious doctrine. As soon as they left, his mother handed him a blue plastic bag with some money and introduced him to a man and said go with him now. She paid the man and never said goodbye. The man didn't talk much, but in his silence was strangely caring. He paid for them to squeeze into the hull of an overcrowded boat that began to sink off the coast. The man and him swam together. If he lagged behind, the man would tread water waiting on him. He got him to Northern France where they separated. He never said goodbye. An English lorry driver smiled at him and opened up the back of his truck. He jumped in with some others. The driver kicked him in the back three times with steel-tipped boots. He does not know why. He does not know why the driver smiled or why he took him across. The driver drove him to England and threw him out at the side of a motorway which he now knows as the M4. He walked to a police station and said *Afghanistan Interpret.*

DAY MOON

For Black Men's Walking group
who walk the Yorkshire Dales.

It beckons, this spirit-filled mist,
like some earthly firmament; this quilted sage
and moss expanse can blank out a racist
boss; its trails will heal our trials and rage.
We hear the cadence of our breaths
and squelched percussion of our boots,
walking beneath these branches bent
into regal arches; talking till we soothe
our too-full minds, we walk for miles.
Next week we'll see the heathers bloom.
Like us, some may forget they thrive
until, watched by this full-day moon,
like ancient rocks lying where they please,
we're couched by this soft earth and these dry weeds.

A JOURNALIST REPEATEDLY ASKS ME ABOUT RACE
IN A POETRY INTERVIEW

So I tell her that my grandmother could curse
more than any sailor. She could drink rum too.
She outdrank big men and she could gamble
on the horses – small outsider bets that would make
her some money. She thought that I was lucky,
so when I went to the bookies to put on a bet for her
she would tell me to put on another bet that I would choose.
I would always win and give her the money.
I was content with being lucky.
She asked me about my poetry and I read her a poem
I was working on at the time, something about ole time mas
and carnival. I recall the first line was about a priest
upset, watching his congregation wine and sweat at carnival.
She told me she had something I could use in my poems –
a report in the newspapers years ago about
an African princess who turned invading English troops
into trees, so they became a forest on the edge of the town.
The strangest thing, she says, is that men in black coats
knocked on her door and demanded the copy of the newspaper;
she watched them through the window, reclaiming all the news.

AND IF I SPEAK OF PARADISE

Then I am speaking about my grandfather
And if I speak of my grandfather
I am speaking about horse racing
And if I speak of horse racing
I am speaking about my father
And if I speak of my father
I am speaking about shirt jacs
And if I speak of shirt jacs
I am speaking about intellectuals
And if I speak of intellectuals
I'm speaking about revolutionaries
And if I speak of revolutionaries
I'm speaking about independence
And if I speak of independence
I'm speaking about Paradise
And if I speak of Paradise…

III

CITIZEN I

For Zena Edwards and her mother

So, after slavery, colonialism, two world wars,
teddy boys, skinheads, rivers of blood speech,
neo-nazis, thatcher, 3 kids, 5 grandkids, a cosy
council house, 20 floors up, a small pension,
now you want to send me home. Oh Woooow!
Even the sandwich van outside the station
selling jerked chicken sandwiches, yet you claim
not to know how they got here. Oh wooowow!
I can buy beef patties at a literary festival in Yorkshire.
Truth is you were always planning my departure,
from the moment I walked down the gangplank,
freestyling "London is the Place for Me".
I notice you wasn't clapping… or smiling.
Can't help thinking this has always been the plan.
In the long game, we've drawn the short jab.
We could hear it in the whispers, even as we
squared your bedsheets and delivered your
blue, veiny kids on the ward. As soon as the labour's
done we could hear as we turned our backs:
Darkie! Sambo! You must think we're dumb.
Are we dumb? From the slaveships to world wars,
to the underground and the hospitals, it's always
been about the labour, never about the living.
Cheap muscles and blood to build you an empire.
It has never been about our living, never about
our tambourine church, our Christmas rum cake,
the audio-science of soundsystems. Our relationship
has never been more than strained at best.
Every second street name is a shout out to my captors.
This one going out to the Wilberforces, who whipped
a little less than the Beckfords. These are the streets
we walk through. We need some black plaques
on these buildings, godammit. Here lived

Florence Scarborough between 1960 and 2005
and, boy, she took noooooooo shit. My gran said,
Let Enoch Powell come to Brixton, talking
that river of blood shit to her face, and he'd be
tasting a river of salty blood in his mouth.
To this day her grandchildren still bring
that rage to the page. So the unspoken question
remains: What to to do with these darkies
after we've wrung them out… AHA. Warm up
them planes, boys, we are returning a cargo called
Windrush generation. What do you mean my dad
can't return from his holiday? The burden of proof
is on us? Again? Think legality and lineage
at the very least. Get the grand kids into a jail or two,
or better yet kill them… in the street, on cctv,
and cellphones, it doesn't matter. It's fine, they think.
These people are an easy target. They do not organise,
centralise or come as one; they've got no major
media outlets, or effective representation in government.
We can send them back for months without
this thing breaking. I smell subterfuge and sleight of hand.
These people keep meticulous records of everything,
even their genocidal imperatives. Hell, I could go
online right now and check on the height, weight,
condition and price of the slaves you brought
and sold in your family, yet our records (poof!)
disappeared. How can you be banished
from your own home? Congratulations.
You fooled us. Render your work, not your lives.
This seems like the newest answer to an old question.
Cheap muscle and blood to build you an Empire –
that we can't stay in. Gran's gone missing from
Saturday morning. Brixton Market? No one is frowning at
the quality of the yams, or asking how the snapper's
eye so cloudy. There'll be no Saturday soup tonight.

CITIZEN II

How is it I'm begging you for housing,
when you burnt my building down?
You all ain't even playing fake-nice, like those
other murderers. You are all cut-eye and snarls,
all straight jargon, and nothing but the jargon.
Can't you smell the ash on me?
I have the stench of cremation.
I can't get it out and I can't get used to it.
It's all well for you,
smelling like pink fabric softener
and aloe vera shampoo.
Ahh, but in your silence you are revealed
through your eyes; look how they blink
in morse code dot dot dot dot
dotdotdot, for I-don't-give-a-fuck.
There is a process, someone says.
What's the process?
Take a number and have a seat.
The number 5 comes up
on a digital sign in red neon;
my ticket number is 25, 000.
When I go to the enquiry desk
and ask to speak to someone
they shout from behind bullet-proof glass:
POOR !!!! then pause for 5 seconds
before shouting BLACK!!!!
So I head back to the hostel,
plotting my next moves in strange equations
on the back of a napkin:
love, love + love + lightning = shout.
I watch static for hours on the black and white
TV with a wire coat-hanger as an antenna.
It looks like electric smoke.
I go to the stove, light a match

and burn it down to my fingers, the flame
burning my fingertips quiet and calm.
I place the wizened match on the counter.
I light another match, turn on the gas.
I squat to look through the fire,
the blue whoosh of the flame.
I light a candle, say a prayer:
Ah you dey in charge of de kingdom,
de power and all de hellish.
I place my hands over the flame,
snuff it out with my thumb and forefinger,
smoke rising from my unsteady hands.

CITIZEN III

Listen up,
you man are on a madness.
Whole estates collapse like Jenga
and memories lie in ruins amongst the rubble.
You man can run this ting if you want to,
but choose to be rats amongst broken stones,
like generations of balding men before you,
seen through open doors of betting shops,
looking at the screens,
ripping up their betting slips.
Men with throbbing veins in their temples,
their jaws clenched, ashamed of their lives.
Through the avenues and sidestreets,
families trembling for their youths
look beyond your neon skyline,
sift the lies out from the truth.
Your mothers and grandmothers worried
about them, but now they fear for you.
Up in glass buildings, men meet
over polished hardwood tables talking to the people
who own your houses and streets,
every reddened brick and crease of mortar,
paving the way for a future that does not include you.
They don't care that you kill each other
once the dead bodies don't get in the way
of the cocktail bars.
Back where you live, people start walking
'round like something missing,
and you youngers don't know what next to do,
so you start clinging to your postcode
like your mothers paid for it,
and you don't want no one round your way,
especially if they look like you,
and if they do, they would feel your danger.

So, suddenly, friends you roll with for years
start get para. Then you defend it,
stand by it, and areas become ends
to be defended from people who look just like you.
So now it all falls down and now it's you lot in the rubble.
You man need to listen up
You man are on a madness.

IV

ON SADE

Sade never liked doing more
than one take of a song.
She thought it unnecessary.
She had been brought up
to avoid the unnecessary.
Her family had not been
very expressive, yet they all
knew there was depth there.
But dramatically sharing –
that was just considered extra.
Everything, even down to what
she wore, was pared back
to the foundations. The engineer
asked *What's the track's name?*
Paradise, she replied.
He asked about the mistakes in her vocal;
she answered, *What mistakes?*

THERE'S NOTHING LIKE THIS: FACTS ABOUT OMAR

Dedicated to Omar

Basquiat placed his painting of a crown on his head. He was part of a five-hundred-year-old soul band call Genealogy. The hoops on each ear are spirit catchers of melody. When he was young he only drank coconut water. His dad recorded the songs he made in kindergarten. He has never had a music lesson except for in dreams. Chords appear to him in colours, so as a youth he could score a summer's day. He's been writing the chord progressions for one song for twenty years. One dream music lesson taught him to sing in the key of Seraphim. He can play every instrument on his albums and a few not on his albums. He sings harmony with himself. He keeps things simple. If you have the money, he's got the music. His tattoos were made with a gramophone record stylus. He was born with golden teeth that he's gradually replaced one by one with enamel.

ASCENSION

For John Coltrane

I heard that as you recorded *Ascension*
your table had a small white cocaine hill.
Through a telescope's dark planetarium
you closed one eye and viewed the world so big,
looking for some language of the heavens.
Snort blow, snort blow, ohhhhhm, we're constellations
inhaled by the night sky, blowing through rhythms
to blue notes, a meditation.
Stars blinking, tiny gods of light,
the world is so vast, but music is bigger.
So this is freedom, so this is your life.
There is no you, just spiralling sounds
pulsing like quasars. Light shooting
up, up, up, upupupupup a celestial chute.
To be a god, sound, is to be moving
the universe, is circular breathing.
Coltrane, Coltrane, look, your nose is bleeding.

THE HUMAN CANVAS
For Mark Rothko

Daylight's seeping through your eyelids
and you're stuck and you want to get up.
It's blood, it's fire, the soft edge of nightmare;
a gaping wound, the gut stink of a battlefield.
It's sacred malice, a slasher movie;
a raw throat, a shout, the tip of the tongue;
death's stain seeping through white sheets.
It's a gaping wound, a canvas of skin peeled back
to coursing capillaries and chunks of fat.
It's a dark sienna of head and heart,
the cerise of a birthing womb,
a coffin's red velvet lining,
a slashed artery gushing like an oil well.
Down the chute of memory
it's something that you forgot
deep in your DNA, a final thought.
All that remains is the taste,
a metallic taste filling your mouth.

STUBB'S WHISTLEJACKET

Looking at Stubb's horse in the dark
it becomes clear he was no glamoriser of muscle,
no fetishist of fur and skin.
Convinced that the body was host
to the horse's spirit, he began making martyrs
of horses, subjecting them to jugular death,
beads of sweat rolling down
their barrelled torsos,
their eyelashes fluttering with a flourish,
as he pumped them with warm tallow
till their pulsing veins and arteries
slowly came to a halt.
Suspending them in a standing or trotting pose
by a series of hooks and tackles,
amid buckets of clotting blood,
first stripping off the skin,
he worked his way through, muscle
by muscle, bone by bone, dissecting
and defining limbs.

Turning the pages in this book of horse,
even in the dark of the museum
I can feel this horse breathing.

THE CHAMPION'S FINAL RUBBING DOWN

The racing crowds had long withdrawn
though my flared wet nostrils still breathed strong,
as my stable boy rubbed down scars and sweat –
the goad of the spur, the cut of the whip.
My trainer talked in whispered breaths:
This is the hour you've outlived your worth.
I will not race again and I know it;
I'm a lowly beast without races to run,
soon to be sold as black market meat,
though racing blood still flows in my veins.
On this heath at Newmarket,
the grass is turning dry, the leaves are brown
and I do not feel like a champion.

PORTRAIT OF MY GREAT GRANDMOTHER AS
THE SUBJECT OF GERICAULT'S *MONOMIE L'ENVIE*

Your mouth is a tense smile or a weak grimace.
Your eyes are tinged with madness.
Barely lit, in your rust-coloured day-dress, in an overcoat
the shade of moss, a frilly bonnet framing your slim face,
your hairline is receding and is now completely silver,
as are your eyebrows, the left one now being raised.
A disapproving thought has flashed through your hot mind.
No doubt you are tired of sitting.
Behind you is darkness, pitch black darkness –
which may be the artist's attempt at a conceit.
But still you are glad each day for the artist's company;
nobody visits you in the asylum now.
Not the panyol Venezuelan carpenter who you fell in love with,
not your children and definitely not your father.
As the respectable owner of many cocoa estates
he wanted this whole damned mess to go away –
a respectable white woman with a poor, brown-skinned Venezuelan
running around the cocoa fields in the moonlight.
He was almost relieved by your madness. It was
the only way he could bring a sense of order back to his name,
though he feared the glitch of your mind would turn up
in future generations, in the odd nephew and a couple of cousins
who, like blown fuses, would start accusing everyone
of wanting to steal their belongings, then stop cleaning
their homes and themselves. But maybe it was also in the women
who preceded you, who'd rather lose people than forgive them,
like you never forgave that Venezuelan carpenter
or anybody else who let you fester in this dark asylum.

A YOUNG GIRL WITH A DOG AND A PAGE
Bartholomew Dandridge, ca. 1725,
Oil on canvas, 48 x 48 inches (121.9 x 121.9 cm)

In the painting you're behind the dog,
an accoutrement like the fermenting grapes
and rotting peaches in the basket that you hold.
You look at her in her lace-trimmed dress
not as a childhood friend, but like
a deity you worship. But there's something
in your acting that speaks of pain;
perhaps because you and the dog
have the same collar; perhaps, not
for the first time, you know you are
less important than the dog.
Even the painter cannot ignore
the wet sadness of your eyes.
He tries to tone it down by lighting
the girl and the dog brightly,
but all that does is make you
a darkness in the background,
a dark and ghostly presence
searing through history.

But I cannot leave you as a ghost,
so I'll name you Quamin from the Akans
and put you in fine blue linen,
place her unlit behind the dog,
an animal collar around her alabaster neck.
You're in a fine hat with a peacock feather,
and I'll have her look at you, in awe.

THE EVER CHANGING DOT

For Stuart Hall

There's an idea, an image in the centre of your forehead,
a dot, like a bindi of the mind. As you talk from your lectern,
images project on the white wall behind, changing as you speak.
Look again at the black athlete on the podium,
deeply veined muscles wrapped in red, white and blue –
standing on an auction block, with his teeth and gums
being checked by the highest bidder's thumb.
Look now at the boy wearing red Adidas. Rhyming
on code wars, territory and where he can and can't go.
Watch a grainy archive film of Lord Kitchener filing
off a gang-plank, singing "London is the place for me".
Think now of Jamaica's ochre sands, where you'd drink
sweet coconut water as a boy. A man in shorts,
with a silver-edged machete, a hotel guide,
is taking you to places you once called home.
Where is home when thinking takes the form of moving on?
Sips of golden rum import memories that change in the telling.
Is home in the shifting memories of the mind,
or in a university hall? Is it in the print of books?
No, too removed. Perhaps it is in the words
of wanderers we feel truly at home.
Look now: a picture of a grey-bearded man, hunched,
typing dense theory in empty, wood-panelled buildings,
someone intervening on his people's behalf,
creating a space and saying "Welcome."

CORBEAUX

But Crow
Crow nailed them
together,
Nailing heaven and
earth together
                    Ted Hughes

As you waddle on earth in your judge's robe guise,
you're a wizened old man, till you float to the sky,
to fly on warm winds with your wings spread wide,

to soar above us all, to surveil with marble eyes
the gut stink of writhing maggots and buzzing flies.
You only circle the clouds when something has died.

As you glide above us like an airborne black scythe
somewhere within us we respect death and its signs,
like you flying on warm winds with your wings spread wide.

As if to make us rejoice in still being alive –
that it is not us or our kin that is in the dust dying –
you only circle the clouds when something has died.

We on the ground carry on with our lives,
because moving on from death is how we're designed,
as you fly on warm winds with your wings spread wide.

By consuming our death, you maintain your life.
Your stained beak drips blood with no regrets,
flying on warm winds with your wings spread wide,
you only circle the clouds when something has died.

MIDWINTER

And crow
is squawking at 6.00 am
in the velveteen black
of a winter morning:
I have already had a cold
morning shower of rain
and fed my offspring
a diet of worms and wet slugs.
Meet the sun before it rises;
master your morning.
Grab that wooden spoon
and stir that gruel
for your family's breakfast.
Master your day,
you lazy human bastard.

THE CROW PALINODE

Human,
I may have been too hard
on you. I did not know
that your young
are often interrupted
in their sleep
and you have been up
attending to your child
in the nights hours.
One of my children
is not right. He does not grow
like the others.
I, like you, am often
sick with worry.
I wake and my mind
is thick with what
feels like spiders' webs.
The others are wondering
what's wrong with their father.
I go through the motions
because they need me,
but it becomes increasingly difficult.
Forgive me, human,
I was too quick in my judgement.
I now understand
the weight you carry.

GIANT MACAJUEL

At first like a hug,
and then, in growing increments,
suffocation, and on to crushing.
I hiss to my prey, *Do not fight.*
Go down easy. Don't be afraid.
This is your fate. Do not shriek.
This is meditation. Slow and painful.
Keep all your energy for final breaths.
Make this transition something to ease into.
Then be taken whole into my mouth.
Isn't this how we take in the world,
one giant mouthful at a time, forcing it down
our gullets as our bellies distend,
till we must lie deathly still
to digest your demise?

What happened here
to this unsuspecting bird
was neither good nor bad.
His bird god must be asleep
or his back turned.
I vomit his bones and feathers
on the grass. The sum total
of our meeting is that I am filled
and he is dead. The snake god
never sleeps; my hugs continue on.

COMPLEXITY

"Popper's remark that despite the non-linear movements of each individual mosquito, the swarm as a whole functions like a coordinated collective is an allusion to the reciprocal effects on complex systems between local behaviors and global outcomes."
— Georg Vrachliotis, "Popper's Mosquito Swarm: Architecture, Cybernetics, and the Operationalization of Complexity".

A high-pitched hum in your ear
as mosquitoes play their bloodlust song,

and I'm outnumbered in insect dusks
trying to smoke them into slumber.

I am humbled by their brave attacks,
their tactics that of underdogs,

like tiny planes around King Kong
who swats and roars at them like thunder.

PARADISE

Is Paradise an island of perfection?
The reward for a life of good deeds,
a payment to the virtuous?
The antidote to hell's fire and brimstone
and endless suffering?
Will there be white sands and crystalline waters,
all pina coladas, swimsuits, shades and sun beds,
our bones finally relaxing in their sun-soaked skins?
Will we see storms far out at sea
that mysteriously never trouble our shores?
And after years in this perfect land,
will we not secretly long for a night
when we wake to skies of bruised clouds,
lightning, a deluge of rain
and a murder of crows
scything the fat-faced acned moon.

V

GRACE

That year we danced to green bleeps on screen.
My son had come early, just the 1kg of him,
all big head, bulging eyes and blue veins.

On the ward I met Grace. A Jamaican senior nurse
who sang pop songs on her shift, like they were hymns.
"Your son feisty. Y'see him just ah pull off the breathing mask."

People spoke of her in half tones down these carbolic halls.
Even the doctors gave way to her, when it comes
to putting a line into my son's nylon thread of a vein.

She'd warn junior doctors with trembling hands: "Me only letting you
        try twice."
On her night shift she pulls my son's incubator into her room,
no matter the tangled confusion of wires and machine.

When the consultant told my wife and I on morning rounds
that he's not sure my son will live, and if he lives he might never
        leave the hospital,
she pulled us quickly aside: "Him have no right to say that
        — just raw so."

Another consultant tells the nurses to stop feeding a baby,
        who will soon die,
and she commands her loyal nurses to feed him. "No baby must dead
wid a hungry belly." And she'd sit in the dark, rocking that
        well-fed baby,

held to her bosom, slowly humming the melody of "Happy" by Pharrell.
And I think, if by some chance, I'm not here and my son's life
        should flicker,
then Grace, she should be the one.

ON NURSES

Surely this is more a calling than a job. The doldrums of the nightshift pierced with the odd life-threatening injury, applying pressure to a gaping wound. Their nurses' shoes clip-clopping down the halls, the thoughts of patients' suffering or dead following them back home. Surely they know that life is random, how death can creep up on the innocent. But how their instincts can sometimes pull spirits back from the brink into their bodies. Like midwives to the spirit. In that moment, do they forget the training and think, if I do this, perhaps they will live? Can you train instinct? I'm not sure. They see it all: the birth, the death, the vomit, the blood, the shock, the diseased, the perturbed, the pain, the smiles. I see them pressing their uniforms for the next shift, washing their hands with a soap that makes their palms peel.

PRAYER

Please. Please save. Please save, dear Lord, my son. My dear son. Lord, Lord, deliver him from pain and allow... allow him to be, allow him to breathe, allow him to join... family. Ours. Hours. My wife. My wife and I await. Anxiously. Await him anxiously... I see him lying. In his incubator. Fighting for his life. Perhaps he does not yet know me yet, Lord, does not know who loves him... his father.

Please make contact. Make contact between mother and child. Skin to skin, let it build bonds. Make comfort, make health. One heartbeat. Swoop downward, swoop, and I would be too tired to fight, to fight the black dog. The black dog's snarl of grief. My churning head. Neon light machines, it's so dark. These babies are alive.

Lord, may mistaken mothers be eased. From guilt from, guilt, dear Lord. Flow breast milk, flow, nectar healing and precious. Son and wife, son and wife, my only focus... Dear Lord, I have cried, I have cursed. I have questioned. Questioned and cursed your judgement. But I know, I know that if it be... be your will, he'd already be. Be dead, a seizure. These miracles of breast milk, oxygen, nurse, incubator means he lives. So there must be some plan. Some bigger plan. So I must, must not, must not lose... faith.

So now I'm praying. Worship prayers, intercession prayers, consecration, commitment and dedication prayers. Comfort my wife, dear Lord, till you deliver our baby to us. Fill all staff, doctors, nurses, cleaners with healing love. Healing love and intuitive, sharp caring. Let their talents and purpose serve your healing spirit. Let blood vessels link organs and provide precious oxygen, nutrients, and cell blood.

Lord, save my baby. Lord, save these babies, save all babies. Lord, save her baby. Lord, save their baby. Lord, save your baby. Once more, amen,
your humble servant till then.

REPAST

With my child fighting every day to live,
the sliver and thin skin of him,
I ate. At first, in celebration he'd lived another day,
but quickly to something else – a hunger
so unsatiable, so rabid.
I took tips from the Indian nurses. Held the softest roti
folded in layers between my fingers,
salivated over pink plastic bowls of beef,
oil-grease floating to the top;
chilli pepper stinging my lips and tongue.
Leaving the hospital car park, with my son alive
another day – no deadly dips in oxygen,
and no sluggish heartbeats –
demanded a celebration. Who knew what we'd face
from the consultant and students on morning rounds –
a bad night, a brain haemorrhage, a death?
Eating felt like a reset, release.
Cooks began to know my first name.
I tried whole menus – saffron-coloured pillau rice,
grains sticking in my beard. I'd clear my wife's plate.
I'd wake unable to sleep, boil four eggs and toast,
half a loaf with butter melting on each slice;
roasted whole chickens stuffed with thyme, and eat
it all, a hunger and thirst like none other;
I'd tongue threads of beef wedged between my teeth,
my lips glistening with ghee.

ON WHISTLING

In our family, we were not allowed
to whistle at night. Our parents said
that it would summon the spirits.
They stopped us, urgently, with panic.
As if their own whistling had once
made something really bad happen,
and they didn't want that for us.
Sometimes I'd look up
at the black night with my lips
pursed, thinking about the spirits
poised to dive like the gargoyles
of Notre Dame.

NOAH

When it rains in the night, it is hard, hard to sleep. He is alert, he is awake, but not afraid, though the hair on his arms is standing on end. He thinks of those left behind. The faces of people he sailed past come to him. How they shouted *Save us* from their rooftops, friends clinging to swaying trees. Horses struggling to remain afloat, desperation in their eyes. Back then he knew that the mandates of God weren't easy. The rain brings them to mind. He puts on his coat and boots and heads towards the barn, feeds the llamas, milks the cows and brushes down the horses. He keeps busy doing what's needed till they come, and he knows they'll come. Then the left behind, or their images, slowly emerge from the forest in varying transparencies of light. Faint shaking dogs spray light out of their fur. Towering, glowing necks of giraffes blow lit puffs of mists from their nostrils. His neighbour has beads of light dripping from his beard. By the hundreds these ghostly animalia come. Noah's shadowy figure looks back at all of them as he contemplates his faith.

SAINTS

Saints are no longer begging to be whipped.
No longer are they *Imitatio Christi*
cloistered behind wall, or shorn of worldly hair.
Saints stand still, bathed in streetlight,
ignoring the poui trees' dropped yellow flowers
and the cars that slow but don't stop.
A saint collects her money up front,
with one breast exposed, at a per-hour
hotel, with a lizard at rest on the windowsill.
A saint is bent over in a car
parked at the beach, chanting a mantra:
Yes uh huh oh baby, baby. Yes uh huh.
The saint looks out the window
at the waves caressing the sand
under a parish of stars.
The saint becomes filled with light,
not from the strokes of her patron,
but by being both present and absent.
The saint knows that a man's musky sweat
can give her a vision of being twelve
and getting her scalp greased in the gallery.
The saint knows that these gifts of vision
are a kind ah heaven right when she needs it,
her heels guiding the foothills of his buttocks.
Saints these days bear other's sweat and suffering.
Saints these days are martyrs to lust.

LIVER

At Jambo, my local barbers,
it's a usual Saturday
with football on the radio
and political debates at shouting level.

Outside, Sadiq is rolling someone
in a hospital wheelchair. Someone a lot thinner
than a grown man is supposed to be;
then we realise it's Abdullah

in standard-issue hospital slippers,
so weak he can't summon his own speech.
Sadiq – his voice – asks how many heads
before Abdullah can get cut.

The whole barber crowd say, Let him cut now.
One of the guys in the barber chair
with half a fade even gets up to let him cut.
But Abdullah is too weak to stand

and Abdi the barber cuts his hair
while he sits in the wheelchair.
Sadiq talks to him to keep his mood
upbeat, but he is too weak to answer.

Sadiq is happy to monologue
as Abdi cuts his hair with the lightest strokes.
The whole barbershop has gone quiet.
They've even turned off the football game.

After the cut Sadiq tries to pay
but Abdi turns his back on him,
says anytime he needs a cut
ring me and I'll help pick him up

from the hospital with the car.
Sadiq offers to pay again.
Abdi calls next.
I ask Abdi if Sadiq and Abdullah

are related and he says, No he's just a friend
taking him out of the hospital
so he can have some normality.
He needs a liver. Time is running out.

SHANDILAY BUSH

After Louise Gluck

When the fevers will not end,
when the doctors with all their study
are silenced, when even your family,
close and extended, are lean with worry,
murmuring fervent prayers within earshot;

when you no longer have enough
energy to raise your body unaided
to sitting position; so weak that
you think that you may not make it past
this day; and you've made peace
with the idea of death, because life
takes an effort that you can no longer summon;

but when you are drenched in sweat
and you can't shake the shivers,
you ignore my bitter taste
as you sip, because by this time
all you want to do is live.

Before I was boiled as your cure
I'd absorbed everything:
nights of full moons, rainy seasons,
nutrients from decomposing dung beetles,
loamy soil, bird song, a list to end your suffering.
I will let you live if you want to live.
I am already drowning your fever as you drink,
your life hanging by my leaves,
your body of fat, skin, blood and bone
all weaker now than my slender stalk.

Drink now, past the dregs to the grit,
and in your mind we are forever
bound; my bitter taste that you once
swore that you couldn't stomach,
you will now sip, and the taste
will come to remind you
of life, of oh sweet sweet life.

MARACAS BEACH PRAYER

With sandy grit, with salt and weeds
each large wave returns to beach.
Make my life this simple, Lord.

The waves consume you where you stand
and feet float up from shallow sand.
Make my life this simple, Lord.

I swim past their crash to gentle seas
and tread still water with my feet.
Make my life this simple, Lord.

Some men pull nets, their veins like streams,
and kids, they kick their ball and scream.
Make my life this simple, Lord.

Of all the gifts you have to give
if this could be a way to live,
make my life this simple, Lord.

A PORTABLE PARADISE

And if I speak of Paradise,
then I'm speaking of my grandmother
who told me to carry it always
on my person, concealed, so
no one else would know but me.
That way they can't steal it, she'd say.
And if life puts you under pressure,
trace its ridges in your pocket,
smell its piney scent on your handkerchief,
hum its anthem under your breath.
And if your stresses are sustained and daily,
get yourself to an empty room – be it hotel,
hostel or hovel – find a lamp
and empty your paradise onto a desk:
your white sands, green hills and fresh fish.
Shine the lamp on it like the fresh hope
of morning, and keep staring at it till you sleep.

ABOUT THE AUTHOR

Roger Robinson is a writer and performer who lives between London and Trinidad. His first full poetry collection, *The Butterfly Hotel*, published by Peepal Tree Press in 2012, was shortlisted for the OCM Bocas Poetry Prize. He has toured extensively with the British Council and is a co-founder of both Spoke Lab and the international writing collective, Malika's Kitchen. He is an alumni of The Complete Works.

Chosen by Decibel as one of 50 writers who have influenced the black-British writing canon over the past 50 years, he has also published a book of short fiction, *Adventures in 3D* (2001); poetry pamphlets *Suitcase* (2004) and *Suckle* (2009). Roger is the lead vocalist for King Midas Sound.

His one-man shows include: *The Shadow Boxer*; *Letter from My Father's Brother*; and *Prohibition* (all premiered at the British Festival of Visual Theatre at Battersea Arts Centre). His duologue show with Nick Makoha, *Mixtape*, has toured nationally and internationally.

In January 2020, Roger Robinson won the 2019 T.S. Eliot prize with *A Portable Paradise*. The Chair of Judges, John Burnside, said this about the collection: "Roger Robinson's characters bear witness to a country where 'every second street name is a shout out to my captors'. Yet though Robinson is unstinting in his irony, he also gives us glimpses of something that his chosen protagonists also refuse to surrender — a taste, through the bitterness, of 'life, of sweet, sweet life'."

ALSO BY ROGER ROBINSON

The Butterfly Hotel
ISBN: 9781845232191; pp. 72; pub. 2013; £8.99

Roger Robinson writes from a place somewhere between Trinidad and Brixton, an insider/outsider vantage point that leads him to see a state of alienation and unbelonging in Black British London that is perhaps no longer so visible to those who have no other world.

Nor can his Trinidad sink into a taken-for-granted familiarity. Its changing reality is all too evident to the periodic returnee, who is conscious of both his growing difference and the fragility of his memories of the world he has known. But these are far from bleak and alienated poems. The very fear of loss generates a drive to recreate the remembered world in all its richness, humour and sensuality. And though the world of the global economy is one that has eroded roots and communities as well as borders, Roger Robinson's poems display a faith in a human capacity for regeneration, of shaping new concepts of home.

Linking and deepening this exploration of this tension between tenacity and fragility is a series of poems that create the world of the butterfly as imagined from within and as observed from without, as metaphor that works at many levels. In moving, pared-down lyrics, expansive prose poems, witty ballads and even a prayer, Roger Robinson's poems are marked by an engagement with the sounds and rhythmic resources of language drawn from both Trinidad and Britain.